For Dzongsar Jamyang Khyentse, Maya, Adelaide, and Oliver.

Special thanks to Carolyn Kanjuro for her editing skills and helping to
bring the Buddha's story to life.

Bala Kids

An imprint of Shambhala Publications, Inc.

4720 Walnut Street

Boulder, Colorado 80301

www.shambhala.com

Text © 2020 by Heather Sanche
Illustrations © 2020 by Tara Di Gesu

9 8 7 6 5 4 3 2 1

First Edition
Printed in China

♾ This edition is printed on acid-free paper that meets the American
National Standards Institute Z39.48 Standard.
♻ Shambhala Publications makes every effort to print on recycled paper.
For more information please visit www.shambhala.com.
Bala Kids is distributed worldwide by Penguin Random House, Inc.,
and its subsidiaries.

Designed by Kara Plikaitis
Hand lettering by Colin Tierney

Library of Congress Cataloging-in-Publication Data
Names: Sanche, Heather, author. | Di Gesu, Tara, illustrator.
Title: The life of the Buddha / Heather Sanche; illustrated by Tara Di Gesu.
Description: First edition. | Boulder: Bala Kids, an imprint of Shambhala
        Publications, Inc. 2020. | Audience: Ages: 3–8. | Audience: Grades: K–3.
Identifiers: LCCN 2019011710 | ISBN 9781611806298 (hardcover: alk. paper)
Subjects: LCSH: Gautama Buddha—Juvenile literature. | Buddhists—
        Biography—Juvenile literature.
Classification: LCC BQ892 .S255 2020 | DDC 294.3/63 [B]—dc23
LC record available at https://lccn.loc.gov/2019011710

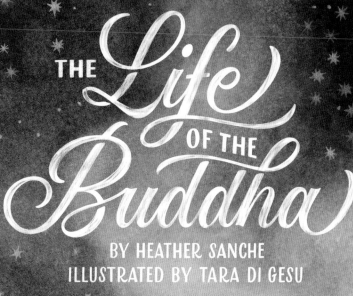

THE Life OF THE Buddha

BY HEATHER SANCHE

ILLUSTRATED BY TARA DI GESU

bala kids

In the full bloom of spring, in a beautiful garden, in a place called Lumbini, a prince was born. His name was Siddhartha. In the middle of that garden stood a wise, old sal tree. Underneath the tree, Prince Siddhartha and his mother Maya sat together, enjoying the cool shade. They both knew the prince had been born at exactly the right time, under the right tree, in the right garden, to the right mother and father.

Soon after his birth, Maya passed away, leaving Siddhartha in the care of her sister, Prajapati. Prajapati loved the young prince with all her heart and raised him tenderly.

When Siddhartha was still very young, a fortune-teller predicted that he would become either a great king or a great spiritual leader. Siddhartha's father, King Shuddhodana, wanted his son to become a king like himself, so he kept the boy inside the palace, giving him all the delights and training befitting a young prince.

And so, the prince grew up surrounded by beautiful toys, delicious food, pleasant companions, and riches of all kinds. An ordinary child might have grown spoiled in that palace, but not Prince Siddhartha.

He was naturally kind and loving to everyone around him. And he was also curious. . . .

A fast and eager learner, Prince Siddhartha quickly absorbed everything he was taught. He excelled at sports and became a master archer. He also composed the finest poetry. But as the years passed, his curiosity grew, and he became more and more restless inside the palace walls. "I wonder what's out there," he often said to himself, sighing.

In time, he married a beautiful maiden, Yashodhara. Together, they had a son named Rahula. One bright afternoon, as the three of them relaxed and played beneath the shade of a rose apple tree, Siddhartha heard a sound unlike anything he had ever heard before—a song filled with sadness, played by a young woman with a sitar. The song drifted on a gentle breeze from far beyond the palace walls and reached right into Siddhartha's heart. He grew perfectly still. His chest ached, and his eyes filled with water like a soft spring rain. He had never felt such a feeling before and longed to understand more about the world that this song came from.

The next day, Siddhartha approached his father and asked,
"May I take my horse for a ride outside the palace walls?"
The king grew dark and said nothing at first. But Siddhartha
insisted.

"All right," said the king, "but take your friend Channa with
you and always stay on the main road."

The king made arrangements so that each time Siddhartha and
Channa went out, all the loveliest young ladies and strongest
young men lined the streets to greet them, just like a parade.
And everyone was truly excited to see the prince.

One day, Siddhartha peeked past the main road, into a quiet alley, where he saw a man with a tired face, wrinkled skin, and a long white beard.

"Who is that?" he asked Channa.

"Oh, that's an old man," Channa answered.

"Will I become old?" asked Siddhartha.

"Yes, everyone becomes old—it's a part of life."

On another outing, Siddhartha peered down a different alley and noticed a man thin and weak, huddled against a building.

"Who is that?" he asked Channa.

"He is a sick man."

"Will I become sick?" asked Siddhartha.

"Yes, everyone becomes sick—it's a part of life."

Next, Siddhartha noticed a man lying in the distance not moving at all.

"Who is that?" he asked Channa.

"He is a dead man."

"Will I die?" asked Siddhartha.

"Yes, everyone dies—it's a part of life."

On their last trip, they passed a man wearing simple saffron-colored robes standing alone on the road. The man had a kind and knowing smile. Although he had nothing more than his simple robes, he looked deeply relaxed and at ease.

"Who is that?" Siddhartha asked.

"He is a sadhu," Channa answered.

"What's a sadhu?"

"A sadhu is a holy man who dedicates his life to searching for the truth."

"Could I become a holy man?" asked Siddhartha.

"You could. Many people give up a normal life to search for the truth."

When they returned to the palace, a great
party had begun with dancing and playing and
feasting of all kinds. But Siddhartha found no
joy in it. He could not forget what he had seen.
He thought about all the lovely ladies and strong
men. He thought about the old man, the sick
man, and the dead man.

That night, while everyone slept, Siddhartha
walked around the palace, deep in thought. As
he gazed at his wife and child, his heart filled
with sadness because he knew that everyone—
no matter how beautiful, how strong, how rich,
or how powerful—would one day experience
old age, sickness, and death. "This is a great and
noble truth," he thought.

More than anything, Siddhartha longed to free everyone from this suffering. Recalling the kind and knowing smile of the sadhu, he decided to leave the comforts of his home in search of the truth that could free people of sorrow. He asked Channa to prepare his horse, and together they left the palace.

As they galloped farther and farther away, Siddhartha knew, deep in his heart, that he had made the right choice.

Soon they came to a river. There, Siddhartha cut off his long hair and put on the simple saffron robes of a holy man. He folded his old clothes carefully and gave them to his friend.

"Channa," he said, "please take these back to my family. Tell them all that I will return once I have discovered how to be free from the suffering of old age, sickness, and death. I promise to share with them what I learn."

Siddhartha wandered for years, far and wide, all across India.

He eventually came upon five holy men who lived in the forest in strict retreat, away from ordinary life. They didn't eat much. They didn't talk much. They didn't bathe much. They never played any games. The five men said that their way could help Siddhartha find the truth of why we suffer and how we can end it, so he decided to join them. But after a while, he became very thin and weak.

One day, a group of girls passed by, singing, laughing, and playing lutes. Siddhartha, hearing their joyful music, realized he had become terribly serious in his search. His body had grown so weak it was like the string of a lute pulled too tightly, ready to break at any moment. "If I continue in this strict way," he thought, "my body may wither away before I find the truth. Then what good will I be?"

He walked down to the river to bathe. One of the girls, Sujata, offered him rice and milk. He ate for the first time in a very long while.

The five holy men looked on and thought, "He has given up his search for the truth."

"Please eat," Siddhartha encouraged them. "Starvation will not help you become free." The holy men said nothing and left Siddhartha by the river.

Strengthened by the food, Siddhartha walked. Not far from the river, he came to an open meadow, near the village of Bodhgaya. In the middle of the meadow stood a huge bodhi tree.

Just then, a grass cutter working in the meadow handed him a bundle of kusa grass. "This grass will make an excellent cushion," thought Siddhartha. And so, he made himself a seat with the grass beneath the bodhi tree and vowed to himself, "I will sit here until I find the truth and become free from suffering."

So he sat.

And sat.

All through the night, Siddhartha's thoughts and feelings came and went. Some were simple and ordinary. Some were fantastically good. And some grew so strong and fierce they loomed like demons in the sky. But Siddhartha did not move. He was not pulled by pleasant thoughts nor harmed by frightening ones. And he discovered the noble truth that the cause of suffering is being attached to feelings and experiences that all come and go.

As the morning star rose in the eastern sky, yet another noble truth dawned in his heart. "There is an end to suffering," he realized, for he himself had gone beyond all suffering. He had become the Buddha, the Awakened One. He knew this, beyond any doubt, and did not need anyone else to tell him it was so. "The earth is my witness," he said. He touched the earth, and the earth trembled.

Seven weeks passed. The Buddha traveled to Sarnath, and once again he met the five holy men in a place called Deer Park. The moment they saw his face—bright, clear, and deeply calm—they knew he hadn't given up his search. He had found true freedom from all suffering.

"Please, tell us what you have discovered," they asked him.

The Buddha shared the first noble truth, that everyone suffers. He shared the second noble truth, the cause of suffering is our attachment. He shared the third noble truth, that there is an end to suffering. Finally, he shared the fourth noble truth. "There is a path, with many methods, that leads to freedom from suffering, and every one of you can take it, just as I have."

The holy men felt inspired by the Buddha's words and became his first students.

Wherever he went, the Buddha taught the path to freedom
from suffering, called the Dharma, to all those he met. And
he kept his promise to his family.

When Prajapati, who had raised him with the tender love of a mother, heard the Dharma, she became the first nun. The Buddha's wife and son also joined the rest of his students to form the community of those who followed the path, and they were called the Sangha. And his father, the king, also found true freedom before he passed away.

The Buddha traveled and taught for forty-five years, and the Sangha grew. As his life neared its end, the Buddha and his community of students gathered in a quiet grove of sal trees near Kushinagar. The Buddha laid down like a lion between two trees and gave a final teaching: "All that is born dies. Dedicate yourselves wholeheartedly to the path of freedom."

Today, there are Buddhists all over the world. Some are monks and nuns. Some are queens and kings. Some have jobs, and many are moms and dads. Wherever you are and whoever you are, you can find a perfect spot, just as the Buddha did, to sit and discover the truth for yourself.

HISTORICAL NOTE

Siddhartha Gautama was born 2,500 years ago as heir to a small North Indian kingdom. Moved by the suffering he witnessed outside his palace walls, he set out on a spiritual journey at the age of twenty-nine. After six years of wandering and meditation, he is said to have become enlightened under the bodhi tree and became known as the Buddha, the Awakened One.

After his enlightenment, the Buddha attracted a following of students and ordained both monks and nuns regardless of their caste or class. His teachings spread and flourished throughout Asia by way of various lineages. As the founder of one of the world's largest religious traditions, Siddhartha Gautama's legacy is that of one of the most influential figures in human history.

Today, Buddhism is prominent in countries such as China, South Korea, Japan, Sri Lanka, Thailand, Nepal, and Bhutan. Buddhism has recently spread throughout the world, and meditation and mindfulness are widely practiced. Buddhist teachings and meditation have also contributed to the fields of philosophy, psychology, ethics, and neuroscience.

The Buddha's life is an example of the capacity we all have within us to realize our innate wisdom and compassion, and a seed of discovery can be sparked for anyone who reads his story.